As the United States rushed to put conventional ground troops into Afghanistan after the September 11 attack, a small group of Afghan rebels working with U.S. special forces and U.S. airpower defeated the Taliban's conventional army and overthrew the regime. Although combining indigenous armies, U.S. special operators, and airpower had been attempted in previous wars, these efforts met with limited success.[1] The speed with which these tactics worked in Afghanistan surprised everyone from National Security Council (NSC) planners to the combatants actively participating in operations.[2] What many of the war's planners had envisioned as a holding operation to prepare the battlefield for a sizable conventional force ended in the rapid defeat of the 50,000 man Afghan army and the fall of the Taliban regime it supported.[3] This new way of war also resulted in a country primarily occupied and policed by indigenous forces.

In view of the problems the U.S. military is experiencing with overextension and the insurgency in Iraq, the Afghan model has much to recommend it. Operations in Afghanistan have cost the United States $54 billion, a sizeable amount, but less than half of the $125 billon spent on Iraq.[4] More importantly, there have been far fewer U.S. casualties in Afghanistan than in Iraq. Through early August, 2005, enemy action has

---

* The views expressed in this article are those of the authors do not necessarily represent the official policy or position of the U.S. Government.

[1] For work on this subject see, for instance, John M. Newman, *JFK and Vietnam: Deception, Intrigue, and the Struggle for Power* (New York: Warner Books, 1992), p. 160; and William Rosenau, *Special Operations Forces and Elusive Enemy Ground Targets: Lessons from Vietnam and the Persian Gulf War* (Santa Monica. Calif.: RAND, 2001).

[2] Bob Woodward records the NSC principals' astonishment on November 12, 2001, to news of the Northern Alliance's unexpected success. See Woodward, *Bush at War* (New York: Simon and Schuster, 2002), particularly p. 306.

[3] William D. Dries, "Future Counterland Operations: Common Lessons from Three Conflicts," master's thesis, U.S. Army School of Advanced Military Studies, 2003, p. 19.

[4] Amy Belasco, *The Cost of Operations in Iraq, Afghanistan, and Enhanced Security*, (Washington, DC: Congressional Research Service, 2005), pp. 1-4.

caused 1,412 deaths in Iraq and only 102 in Afghanistan.[5] Beyond this, unlike Iraq, Afghanistan has become sufficiently stable to allow the presence of U.N. personnel for reconstruction efforts.[6] Afghanistan's relative stability is all the more remarkable given that Afghanistan has a larger population, terrain more suited to guerillas, and a tradition of warlords with independent armies. Thus, the Afghan model suggests a less costly and more effective method of accomplishing US security objectives.[7]

This optimistic view of the utility of the Afghan model in U.S. foreign policy, however, holds up only so long as the tactical and operational techniques used in Afghanistan can work elsewhere. Despite the success of the model in Afghanistan, analysts have argued that precision airpower has not changed the fundamental calculus of ground warfare and have offered a number of alternative explanations for success. After the fall of the Taliban, politicians and academics alike suggested that the model could succeed only in circumstances exactly like those found in Afghanistan. U.S. Secretary of State Colin Powell, speaking in December 2001, warned that the model would not work in Iraq; other analysts asserted that the model would not work "in major regional contingencies."[8] Writing from a tactical perspective, Stephen Biddle argues that the new form of air operations merely constitutes an incremental increase in airpower's capability

---

[5] Global War on Terrorism Casualties, Defense Manpower Data Center, Statistical Information Analysis Division. Hostile deaths include killed in action, died of wounds, died while missing in action, and died while captured. Non-hostile deaths are categorized as accident, illness, homicide, self-inflicted, undermined, and pending final determination.

[6] Secretary-General Report to the UN Security Council on the Situation in Afghanistan and its Implications for International Peace and Security, 18 March 2005.

[7] Currently there are about 140,000 US troops in Iraq and only about 20,000 in Afghanistan. http://www.globalsecurity.org/military/ops/iraq_orbat.htm

[8] Secretary of State Colin Powell, quoted in Eric Schmitt and James Dao, "Use of Air Power Comes of Age in New War," *New York Times*, December 24, 2001. Milan Vego, "What Can We Learn from Enduring Freedom?" U.S. *Naval Institute Proceedings*, vol. 128, No 7 (July 2002), pp. 28-33.

in the century-old contest between the lethality of weapons and the dispersion of ground troops. Although the new weapons and tactics took Taliban troops by surprise, they quickly compensated for the unanticipated lethality of new U.S. guided bombs by dispersing, camouflaging themselves, and digging in. Once that point was reached, victory depended principally on the training of the respective ground forces.[9] In short, precision airpower was marginally helpful, but the new way of war depended on the skill levels of the troops supported by U.S. airpower. Unskilled rebels could not defeat trained conventional forces.[10] In a different vein, Michael O'Hanlon argues that, although the new airpower-intensive methods are tremendously useful, they cannot substitute for U.S. troops because foreign forces cannot be expected to fight consistently for U.S. military objectives. In Afghanistan, he argues, the groups the United States supported were effective only as long as the United States pursued regime change. Later, when the United States attempted to induce them to hunt surviving members of al-Qaida as they fled, Afghan allies proved unreliable. Thus, despite his praise for the Afghan campaign, like Biddle, O'Hanlon concludes that the model will seldom provide a substitute for deploying heavy concentrations of U.S. troops.[11] Variations of both Biddle's and

---

[9] Stephen Biddle, "Afghanistan and the Future of Warfare," *Foreign Affairs*, Vol. 82, No. 2 (Mar/Apr 2003), p. 31. For a more detailed explanation of this argument see Stephen Biddle, *Special Forces and the Future of Warfare: Will SOF Predominate in 2020* (Carlisle Pa, Strategic Studies Institute: U.S. Army War College, 2004), p. 14; and Stephen Biddle, *Afghanistan and the Future of Warfare: Implications for Army and Defense Policy* (Carlisle Pa, Strategic Studies Institute: U.S. Army War College, 2002).

[10] Biddle, *Special Forces and the Future of Warfare*, p. 17. For a theoretical explication of this argument see Stephen Biddle, "The Past as Prologue: Assessing Theories of Future Warfare," *Security Studies*, Vol. 8, No. 1 (Autumn 1998), pp. 1-74, especially pp. 24-26; Conrad C. Crane, *The U.S. Army's Initial Impressions of Operations Enduring Freedom and Noble Eagle* (Carlisle, Pa.: U.S. Army War College, 2002).

[11]Michael E. O'Hanlon, "A Flawed Masterpiece," *Foreign Affairs*, Vol. 81 No. 3 (May/June 2002), pp. 54-57. For detailed historical accounts, see Philip Smucker, *Al Qaeda's Great Escape: The Military and the Media on Terror's Trail* (Washington, D.C.: Brassey's., 2004); Susan B. Glasser, "The Battle of Tora Bora: Secrets, Money, Mistrust," *Washington Post*, February 10, 2002; John Donnelly, "Fighting Terror/The Military Campaign; How U.S. Strategy in Tora Bora Failed, Deals by Afghan Allies May Have Let al qaida

O'Hanlon's arguments have been reflected widely in the professional and academic literature.[12]

In this article, we argue that the pessimism that has characterized analysis of the Afghan model is misplaced. Air power, special forces, and indigenous troops (even those with relatively little training) form a powerful and robust combination. While events in Afghanistan and later in northern Iraq demonstrated the costs and the benefits to using the model, when these are compared with the costs and benefits of deploying heavy divisions, and particularly the costs of creating new governments without indigenous war allies, the model performs well. Moreover, because this new way of war lowers the costs to the United States, in both blood and treasure, it creates a more credible stick to use in coercive diplomacy against small—and medium—sized opponents than threats of conventional invasion. The lesson of Afghanistan and Iraq is that, when used correctly, the Afghan model offers the United States strategic advantage and leverage abroad.

Below we analyze how this new way of war performed in Afghanistan and later in Iraq. The study explores how the techniques came about in the face of a largely skeptical military establishment, why they worked, and some of their strengths and weaknesses.

Leaders Escape," *Boston Globe*, February 10, 2002; Martin Arostegui, "The Search for bin Laden," *Insight Magazine*, August 12, 2002, http://www.insightmag.com/news/2002/09/02/World/Special.Reportthe.Search.For.Osama.Bin.Laden-260506.shtml; Benjamin Lambeth, *"Air Power against Terror: An Assessment of Operation Enduring Freedom,"* forthcoming.

[12] William R. Hawkins, "What Not to Learn from Afghanistan," *Parameters*, Vol. 32, No. 2 (Summer 2002), pp. 24-32, 31; Doug Mason, "A New American Way of War? Identifying Operational Lessons from American Involvement in Southwest Asia, Kosovo, and Afghanistan" Joint Military Operations Department, Naval War College (February, 2002), p. 11; John Hendren, "Afghanistan Yields Lessons for Pentagon's Next Targets," *Los Angeles Times*, Jan 21. 2002; Michael Gordon, "One War, Differing Aims," *New York Times*, December 18, 2001; Michael R Lwin, "Coherent Joint Warfare Is Our Silver Bullet," *Proceedings*, Vol. 129, No. 10 (October 2003), pp. 56-59; Timothy R. Reese, "Precision Firepower: Smart Bombs, Dumb Strategy," *Military Review*, Vol. 83, No. 4 (July-August 2003), pp. 46-53, 48; and Max Boot, "The New American Way of War," *Foreign Affairs*, Vol. 82, No. 4, (July/August 2003), pp. 41-58.

We conclude with a discussion of the strategic implications of the model for future U.S. military diplomacy.

The Afghan Model

The military operation the United States conducted to overthrow the Taliban regime in Afghanistan in 2001 represents something new in warfare. After the war, analysts, searching for a label, termed the operations the "Afghan model" and "the new way of war."[13] In the model, U.S. airpower degrades enemy communications throughout the theater of war. Then, U.S. special forces use light indigenous troops as a screen against enemy infantry and force the enemy to mass before calling in precision air strikes.[14] Although these operations proved enormously successful in Afghanistan, before the war few military thinkers had much confidence that they could work.

PLANNING OPERATIONS FOR AFGHANISTAN

Planning for military operations in Afghanistan took place in the shadow of one of the more acrimonious theoretical debates over military affairs in U.S. history. While the dispute had long-standing roots, U.S. airpower's unanticipated battlefield success during the 1991 Persian Gulf War revived the argument over its role on the modern battlefield.

---

[13] For more information on these names, see: Boot, "The New American Way of War"; and Biddle, "Afghanistan and the Future of Warfare."

[14] Paul L. Hastert, "Operation Anaconda: Perception Meets Reality in the Hills of Afghanistan," *Studies in Conflict & Terrorism*, Vol. 28, No. 1 (January 2005), p. 11; Kim Burger, "Afghanistan: First Lessons," *Jane's Defence Weekly*, December 19, 2001; Ann Scott Tyson, "U.S. Is Prevailing with Its Most Finely Tuned War," *Christian Science Monitor*, November 21, 2001, p. 1; Paul Watson and Richard Cooper, "Blended Tactics Paved Way for Sudden Collapse," *Los Angeles Times*, November 15, 2001; Michael Gordon, "'New' U.S. War: Commandos, Airstrikes, and Allies on the Ground," *New York Times*, December 29, 2001; Thom Shanker, "Conduct of War Is Redefined by Success of Special Forces," *New York Times*, January 21, 2002; Hendren, "Afghanistan Yields Lessons for Pentagon's Next Targets," p. 1; and Joseph Fitchett, "Swift Success for High-Tech Arms," *International Herald Tribune*, December 7, 2001.

The debate pitted ground power anti technologists, who argued that technology had not affected the basic characteristics of the air-ground operations since World War I, against airpower technophiles, who proposed that airpower's new capabilities largely removed the need for ground troops in contemporary warfare.[15] Realistically, however, the debate revolved around questions about how best to use airpower's new precision and stealth capabilities against enemy fielded forces.[16] The most politically charged issue involved how many fewer U.S. ground troops would be needed to accomplish the same objectives given airpower's new capabilities. If the airpower advantage was large, technophiles believed and technophobes feared, fewer ground troops would be required in future wars, which might mean larger budgets for the special forces and close air support (CAS) platforms and smaller allocations for the traditional army and air force programs.[17]

---

[15] Biddle argues that the "real causes of battlefield success have been surprisingly stable since 1917-1918"; he goes on to say that "expectations of a looming revolution in military affairs are both a serious misreading of modern military history and a dangerous prescription for today's defense policy: they could easily lead to an overemphasis on new technology or radical operational concepts that could weaken, not strengthen, the American military and undermine its ability to prevail on future battlefields." Stephen Biddle, *Military Power: Explaining Victory and Defeat in Modern Battle* (Princeton, N.J.: Princeton University Press, 2004), p. ix. For an opposing view, see John A. Warden III, "Employing Air Power in the Twenty-first Century," in Richard H. Schultz, Jr. and Robert L. Pfaltzgraff Jr. eds., *The Future of Air Power in the Aftermath of the Gulf War* (Maxwell Air Force Base, Al: Air University Press, 1992), pp. 57-83.

[16] Benjamin S. Lambeth argues that the rhetoric surrounding the debate has masked the real issue which is how new technologies are changing the use of air assets in ground operations. Lambeth, *The Transformation of American Air Power* (Ithaca, N.Y.: Cornell University Press, 2000). See also Tony Mason, *Air Power: A Centennial Appraisal* (Washington D.C.: Brassey's, 1994); and Robert A. Pape, "The True Worth of Airpower," *Foreign Affairs*, Vol. 83, No. 2 (March/April 2004), pp. 116-130.

[17] See Lambeth, *The Transformation of American Air Power*; Daryl G. Press, "The Myth of Air Power in the Persian Gulf War and the Future of Warfare," *International Security*, Vol. 26, No. 2 (Fall 2001), pp. 5-44; Stephen Biddle, "Victory Misunderstood: What the Gulf War Tells Us about the Future of Conflict," *International Security,* Vol 21, No. 2 (Fall 1996), pp. 139-179; Stephen Biddle, "Assessing Theories of Future Warfare," Paper Presented to the 1997 Annual Meeting of the American Political Science Association, Washington, D.C., August 1997; James R. Blaker, "Understanding the Revolution in Military Affairs: A Guide to America's 21st Century Defense," Working Paper No. 3 (Washington , D.C.: Progressive Policy Institute); Michael G. Vickers, "Warfare in 2020: A Primer" (Washington, D.C.: Center for Strategic and Budgetary Assessments, 1996); Biddle, "Afghanistan and the Future of Warfare," p. 3; Hunter Keeter, "Anti-Terror Campaign Could Speed Military Transformation," *Defense Daily*, November 21, 2001, p. 4; Michael Vickers, "The 2001 Quadrennial Defense Review, the FY 2003 Defense Budget

In the wake of the September 11 terrorist attacks, this question moved from the theoretical to the practical when President George W. Bush asked the NSC for plans to remove the Taliban regime by force.[18] In response, the NSC outlined two plans. The more conventional plan, presented by the Joint Chiefs of Staff, required several army divisions and months of preparation.[19] The second option, proposed by the CIA, called for rapidly taking down the Taliban regime through a combination of airpower, U.S. special operations forces (SOF), and Afghan rebels.[20]

Given previous experiences with special operations, it is hardly surprising that seasoned military planners balked at the CIA's proposal. Airpower has been partnered with special operations forces many times; however, never before had the two played the main effort in a war.[21] The best example of the type of campaign the CIA was

---

Request and the Way Ahead for Transformation: Meeting the 'Rumsfeld Test'" (Washington, DC: Center for Strategic and Budgetary Analysis, June 19, 2002).

[18] Investigators quickly established that the attacks had been carried out by members of al-Qaida, a group aided by the Afghan government.

[19] Woodward, *Bush at War*, p. 291. An early version of the plan, sometimes dubbed the standard "forty-eight months and five divisions," is described in Daniel Benjamin and Steven Simon, *The Age of Sacred Terror: Radical Islam's War against America* (New York: Random House, 2003), p. 295.

[20] The CIA had carefully cultivated contacts with Afghan rebels in the preceding years. In the months before September 11, the agency had proposed increasing aid to the Northern Alliance in hopes of deposing the Taliban. Schroen offers perhaps the best account of the early stages of Operation Enduring Freedom. Gary C. Schroen, *First In: An Insider's Account of How the CIA Spearheaded the War on Terror in Afghanistan* (New York: Ballantine Books, 2005). See also Woodward, *Bush at War*. For a wider political view of America's thinking on methods of dealing with terrorists in Afghanistan, see Benjamin and Simon *The Age of Sacred Terror,* pp. 326-349.

[21] SOF and airpower saw extensive use during WWII. In the European and Mediterranean Theaters aircraft inserted and extracted intelligence agents on clandestine missions and dropped supplies to resistance fighters. Robert Jackson, *The Secret Squadrons*, (London, Robson Books Ltd., 1983), pp. 112-119; Bernard V. Moore, II, "'The Secret Air War Over France' USAAF Special Operations Units in the French Campaign of 1944, master's thesis, School of Advanced Airpower Studies, Maxwell AFB, Ala., 1992. In the Pacific theater an air unit was established to transport and supply specialized infantry units working behind the Japanese lines in Burma. Airmen also flew fighter and bomber missions, providing the ground forces with added firepower. Philip D. Chinnery, *Any Time, Any Place: Fifty Years of the USAF Air Commandos and Special Operations Forces, 1944-1994* (Annapolis, Md.: Naval Institute Press, 1994), pp. 14-59; David M. Sullivan, "From Burma to Baghdad: Enhancing the Synergy between Land-Based Special Forces and Combat Air Operations," master's thesis, School of Advanced Air and Space Studies, Maxwell AFB, Ala., 2003, pp. 28-34

suggesting for Afghanistan occurred during the Vietnam War when a combination of SOF, airpower, and indigenous tribal allies were used to combat the infiltration of troops and supplies from North Vietnam along the Ho Chi Minh trail through Laos and Cambodia. During that campaign, the United States teamed special forces with paramilitary units of ethnic minorities such as the Montagnard and Nung tribesmen to collect intelligence and pinpoint targets. For the most part, these forces attempted to avoid the enemy when possible. In the end, these operations proved risky for SOF operators and limited in their ability to destroy enemy forces. [22]

Yet there were reasons to think the model might work better now. In the years since the end of the Vietnam War, and especially after Desert Storm, the proliferation of new technology had significantly enhanced the capabilities of both SOF and air power and began to change the relationship between the two. Portable laser designators, for example, enabled teams to direct laser-guided weapons dropped from aircraft overhead. The Global Positioning System (GPS), in addition to enhancing navigation (and therefore survivability), allowed teams to pass accurate target coordinates to orbiting aircraft. Together, these tools provided SOF forces with enhanced stealth and force application capabilities far beyond those of their Vietnam-era predecessors. By 2001, special operators had come to believe that the fusion of better information and increased accuracy of precision-guided munitions (PGM) would allow small teams to achieve lethality on a scale unimaginable just a few years earlier. Nevertheless, these trends had

---

[22]Initial plans called for large-scale operations using thousands of recruited Laotian tribesman, but political considerations restricted the missions to small teams. Rosenau, *Special Operations Forces and Elusive Enemy Ground Targets: Lessons from Vietnam and the Persian Gulf War*; Sullivan, pp. 47-56; John L. Plaster, *SOG: The Secret Wars of America's Commandos in Vietnam* (New York: Simon & Schuster, 1997), ff; United States Air Force, "Project CHECO: USAF Support of Special Forces in SEA," March 1969.

not seen large-scale testing on the battlefield and remained mainly theoretical. Beyond this, they had gone largely unnoticed outside the SOF community. Perceptions of air power integration in special operations continued to focus on transportation, CAS, and occasional air power support for direct attack missions using dedicated special operations air assets. Although the notion of SOF directing air in support of indigenous allies was an accepted historical fact, few, even among the special forces, could imagine a time when this would constitute the main effort in a sustained campaign.

Despite the prevailing military opinion about the utility of a SOF-heavy campaign, President Bush selected the plan proposed by the CIA rather than the one offered by the Joint Chiefs. The reasons for this are not hard to fathom. In the first place, emotions in the country ran high, and there was intense pressure to avenge the bloodiest attack on U.S. soil since Pearl Harbor.[23] More practically, however, U.S. decision makers faced significant geographical and diplomatic obstacles to mounting a heavy conventional operation in Afghanistan. As one army planner commented, landlocked and diplomatically isolated Afghanistan is "the most strategically impossible place to introduce force on the entire . . . planet."[24] Realistically, there was no way to project large numbers of ground troops to the region quickly.[25]

Beyond these considerations, however, loomed the larger strategic fear among some that a successful invasion of Afghanistan by U.S. forces was likely to lead to a prolonged guerrilla war. As repeated recorded conversations attest, President Bush and

---

[23] Evidence of this pressure was visible in a National Security Council meeting ten days after the attacks, when President Bush noted "We've got to start showing results." Quoted in Woodward, *Bush at War*, p. 113.

[24] Interview with Col. Mark Rosengard, director of operations, Task Force Dagger, by Major Mark Davis, School of Advanced Air and Space Studies, Maxwell Air Force Base, Alabama., February 27, 2004.

[25] Vego, "What Can We Learn from Enduring Freedom?"

members of his cabinet were well aware of Afghanistan's reputation as "the graveyard of empires" and feared a U.S.-lead invasion would result in a guerrilla war.[26] Most recently, the Soviet Union had lost thousands of lives and spent billions of rubles fighting a losing war against Afghan insurgents during the 1980s. Both the fiercely independent character of indigenous tribes and the mountainous geography made the prospects of an insurgency against an occupying U.S. army likely.[27] Bob Woodward concisely describes the administration's dilemma, "If the U.S. repeated the mistakes of the Soviets by invading with a large land force, they would be doomed." [28]

Interestingly, the belief that a U.S. invasion would lead to a guerrilla war was not unique to American strategists. The leaders of the Taliban and al-Qaida shared a common strategic picture with American policymakers. Like many others, they had read the military lesson of the 1990s as saying that airpower was overrated and that the United States would need to use heavy ground forces to bring down the regime. In their view, this necessity played into their hands.[29]

In the weeks of diplomacy that preceded military action, Afghanistan's leader, Mullah Omar, and al-Qaida's Osama bin Laden appear to have devised a two-pronged strategy. Omar attempted to use the time it would take to insert U.S. troops into Afghanistan to break up the coalition the United States would need to take action against

---

[26] Woodward, *Bush at War*, pp. 82, 131, 182, 193.

[27] Afghanistan has long been the bane of invading armies; Alexander the Great struggled there, and Britain's attempts to subdue the region failed miserably. See Milton Bearden, "Afghanistan: Graveyard of Empires," *Foreign Affairs*, Vol. 80, No. 6 (November/December 2001), pp. 13-30.

[28] Woodward, *Bush at War*, p. 193.

[29] Bin Laden's scorn of U.S. airpower appears in numerous speeches, particularly after the unsuccessful cruise missile attack on al-Qaida's Afghan training camps following the 1998 bombings of the U.S. embassies in Kenya and Tanzania. See, for instance, "Exclusive Interview: Conversation with Terror," *Time Asia,* September 14, 2001, http://www.time.com/time/asia/news/interview/0,9754,174550,00.html.

his landlocked country. Throughout the period, and during the war, pro-Taliban protests

and riots became a frequent occurrence in neighboring Pakistan.[30] A massive

deployment of U.S. troops through that country would have significantly exacerbated

these effects. How long the pro-U.S. regime could have held out against its increasingly

anti-U.S. population is unclear.[31]

The second part of the strategy was conducted by al-Qaida and closely mirrored

President Bush's chief fear. According to bin Laden, a war between the United States

and Afghanistan could be turned into a global victory for al-Qaida if it turned the people

of the Muslim world against the United States. His speeches revealed a calculated

strategy to pull the United States into a guerrilla war in Afghanistan. In a taped speech

released to the al-Jazeera satellite network on October 7, 2001, bin Laden taunted the

United States to attack. He argued that if it sent troops into Afghanistan, the Taliban

would use the same tactics against them as they had used to defeat the Soviet Union; in

addition, a prolonged war that involved atrocities against Muslims would energize

Islamic nations to overthrow their conservative governments and would drain the

willingness of the U.S. public to project power into the Middle East.[32] In short, bin

Laden saw the U.S. plan to inject troops into Afghanistan as leading to a victory not only

---

[30] See for instance: Michael A. Lev, "Pakistan Quells Anti-U.S. Protests," *Chicago Tribune*, October 9, 2001; "Protests Rock Pakistan," *Guardian Unlimited*, Friday September 21, 2001, http://www.guardian.co.uk/wtccrash/story/0,1300,555779,00.html.

[31] Woodward relates some of the conversations between NCS principals regarding this problem. Woodward, *Bush at War*, pp. 58-9, 82, 123, 173.

[32] For an analysis of al-Qaida's strategy taken from bin Laden's speeches before and during Operation Enduring Freedom, see: Ronald E. Zimmerman, "Strategic Provocation: Explaining Terrorist Attacks on America," masters thesis, School of Advanced Air and Space Studies, Maxwell Air Force Base, 2002. The strategy was first clearly articulated by bin Laden in a speech in August 1996. "Osama bin Laden vs. the US: Edicts and Statements." Frontline, April 1995, http://www.pbs.org/wgbh/pages/frontline/shows/binladen/who/edicts.html.

for his followers in that country, but in the entire Muslim world.[33] The similiarity between bin Laden's plan and the thinking of the Bush administration shows a remarkable coincidence of strategic logic across vastly disparate audiences.

THE SURPRISING SUCCESS OF THE AFGHAN CAMPAIGN

Operation Enduring Freedom began with a marked lack of coordination between SOF and airpower. Although a daring CIA team rapidly established links with rebels in northern Afghanistan, it took much longer to insert the special forces that would be needed to support the warlords and call in air strikes.[34] Moreover, neither the NSC nor the armed forces had a clear idea about how the campaign should unfold and weeks more went by as the president's team debated whether helping the Northern Alliance's ethnic Tajiks and Uzbecs—in a predominantly Pashtun country—would cause more political problems after the war than their battlefield potential warranted.[35] Beyond this, apparently, the army saw the campaign as a means of preparing the battlefield for heavy U.S. troops, and it is not clear whether the air force and navy had specific plans to coordinate with ground troops, U.S. or otherwise.[36]

As regards the air campaign at the beginning of OEF, most analyses have focused on the relative paucity of fixed targets in Afghanistan and the fact that airpower destroyed the vast majority of these targets in the first few days of the campaign. Less noted, however, is the effect of airpower on Taliban troops. Having destroyed the Taliban's

---

[33] Zimmerman, "Strategic Provocation."

[34] For a comprehensive account of CIA operations in Afghanistan in the wake of after September 11, see Schroen, *First In*.

[35] For more on this debate see Woodward, *Bush at War*, pp. 266, 280.

[36] Dries, "Future Counterland Operations," p. 19.

high-value fixed targets, airpower rapidly shifted to the fielded forces.[37] Although these

attacks met with a good deal of initial success, Taliban forces quickly adapted by

dispersing troops into small units that were hard to spot from the air and, more

importantly, difficult to distinguish from civilians.[38] While these tactics afforded a level

of protection from air-attacks, in adopting these tactics the Taliban troops lost most of

their ability to conduct conventional operations, rendering them all but ineffective in their

main mission of fighting rebel forces. Thus, airpower effectively removed these forces

from the field.[39]

As the Taliban troops along the northern frontier dispersed, however, increasing

activity by Northern Alliance forces, particularly those of Northern Alliance General

Abdurrashid Dostum, forced the Taliban to take a different approach. Facing opposing

ground forces, Taliban commanders chose to mass to defend some areas, relying heavily

on trenches for protection. Like their dispersal tactics in the south, these methods blunted

U.S. airpower.[40]

By late October, less than a month into the campaign, clear signs of public

restlessness began to appear as the terms "stalemate" and "quagmire" started to surface in

media accounts of the war. Noted airpower theorist Robert Pape argued that the U.S. air

---

[37] Interview with Col. Tom Ehrhard, chief of the combined air operations center strategy division during Operation Enduring Freedom. School of Advanced Air and Space Studies, April 4, 2005.

[38] Biddle, "Afghanistan and the Future of Warfare."

[39] Interview with Col. Ehrhard.

[40] At an NSC meeting on October 15, Secretary of Defense Donald Rumsfeld argued that the main problem in the Shamali plains was finding the enemy. In Mazar and Konduz, the enemy was located but how well their entrenchments worked before SOF designators arrived is an open question. Throughout October, air did not concentrate much effort on the entrenched Taliban, Arab, and Pakistani volunteer forces arrayed in these areas. Woodward, *Bush at War*, pp. 240, 264.

strategy was not working.[41] Peter Beaumont's report that "the war had become bogged down" typified press reports of the period.[42] Others told Americans to expect tough resistance from a "hard core of Taliban leaders."[43]

Even as these opinions emerged the conduct of the fighting was changing. On October 19, 2001, with the air war stagnating and political pressure for results mounting, Secretary of Defense Donald Rumsfeld announced that U.S. troops would give direct assistance to Afghan opposition groups.[44] Two days later, SOF personnel called in their first air strikes in support of the Northern Alliance's advance toward Mazar-e-Sharif.[45] Those attacks signaled the end of the traditional relationship between SOF and airpower and the emergence of the "Afghan model."

The addition of SOF-directed precision airpower transformed the campaign by radically improving the ability of airpower to destroy the Taliban's fielded forces; once the new tactics were brought to bear, Taliban forces were quickly overwhelmed. Major combat actions using the new model began when Dostum's forces conquered the village of Bishqab. By the end of October, 80 percent of the air effort was dedicated to backing opposition forces in Afghanistan, and the Bush administration publicly acknowledged that SOF were working directly in support of the Northern Alliance.[46] A rapid succession of victories followed in November: Bai Beche fell on the fifth, Mazar-e-Sharif on the

[41] Robert Pape, "The Wrong Battle Plan," *Washington Post*, October 19, 2001.

[42] Peter Beaumont, et al., "The Rout of the Taliban," *Observer Special Reports*, November 18, 2001, available from http://observer.guardian.co.uk/afghanistan/story/0,1501,596923,00.html. See, R.W. Apple Jr., "A Military Quagmire Remembered: Afghanistan as Vietnam," *New York Times,* October 31, 2001.

[43] Ahmed Rashid, "Inside the Taliban," *Far Eastern Economic Review*, October 28, 2001, p. 21.

[44] David R Brooks, *Case Study: The First Year: US Army Forces Central Command during Operation Enduring Freedom* (Carlisle Pa: US Army War College, 2002), p. 30.

[45] Ibid. For a detailed account see Schroen, *First in.*

[46] Thomas E. Ricks and Doug Struck, "US Troops Coordinating Airstrikes," *Washington Post*, October 31, 2001.

tenth, Kabul on the thirteenth, and Konduz on the twenty-sixth. In dramatic fashion,

within a few days of beginning to employ the new method, friendly forces had gained

control of nearly half the country. On December 6, just sixty days after the start of the

war, Mullah Omar and senior Taliban officials abandoned Kandahar and went into

hiding, effectively terminating Taliban administration of Afghanistan.[47]

WHY THE AFGHAN CAMPAIGN SUCCEEDED

According to conventional military wisdom, the types of operations employed in OEF

should not have worked. When used on the tactical offense, special operations forces

screened by lightly armed indigenous troops should have been rapidly destroyed by the

Taliban's conventional army. Yet they were not. The operations succeeded in

Afghanistan because of a combination of interrelated tactical—and operational—level

dynamics. The unexpected outcome did not occur because of a particular technology or

tactic; rather the synergy of a series of new capabilities transformed the nature of the

campaign into something new and revolutionary.[48]

Traditional combined arms warfare has been the central paradigm in conventional

war for the last century, and its dynamics are well understood. In this type of war, the

central tension exists between concentration and dispersal. In the forward areas, troops

disperse and entrench to avoid lethal fire from automatic weapons and artillery. In rear

areas, troops concentrate along roads and other lines of communication to facilitate the

movement of supplies and reserves to the front. The overall goal for both sides is to

[47] Andrew J. Birtle, "Afghan War Chronology" (Washington, DC: U.S. Army Center of Military History Information Paper, March 22, 2002), pp. 8.

[48] The level of analysis in examining the Afghan model is important. Stephen Biddle's work on the subject examines the tactical level and, consequently, overlooks the synergy between air and ground that is at the heart of the new model. On why he examines the tactical level, see Biddle, "Afghanistan and the Future of Warfare," p. 25, particularly n 59.

break through the enemy's front line, to secure a salient, and to exploit massed enemy assets in its lightly defended rear areas.[49] (Cutting these lines is critical because isolating an army from its lines of communication greatly degrades its ability to fight.)[50] Achieving this goal, however, is difficult. Dug-in defenders with automatic weapons enjoy a significant tactical advantage over attackers moving forward without cover. To overcome this advantage, attackers concentrate their forces such that they have a significant numerical advantage over defenders at the point of the breakthrough.[51]

The Afghan model worked for two key reasons. The first occurred in the early days of the campaign when theater-wide bombing forced the Taliban to disperse into small groups that did not move in the open. The second reason, however, is less straightforward and requires an understanding of how dispersed and entrenched defenders traditionally overcome the attacker's greater numbers and massed artillery fires. On a tactical level, dispersed defenders rely on cover and concealment for protection. Although these measures offer a good defense against artillery, the dispersion makes the defender vulnerable to a massed infantry attack by a committed attacker supported by artillery. More important against such a combined arms attack are operational-level dynamics.

Defenders make use of three particularly effective operational level defenses. First, they arrange their forces in depth, forcing the attackers to go through more of the defender's frontline forces. The arrangement causes the attackers to extend their lines of

---

[49] For a breakdown of other goals in conventional war see John J. Mearsheimer, *Conventional Deterrence* (Ithaca N.Y.: Cornell University Press, 1983), chap. 2, 6.

[50] See B.H. Liddell Hart, *The Memoirs of Captain Liddell Hart*, Vol. 1 (Cassell & Co.: London, 1965), pp. 41-49; Biddle, *Military Power: Explaining Victory and Defeat in Modern Battle*, p. 41.

[51] For a more detailed theoretical analysis of tactics, Liddell Hart, *Memoirs*, Vol. 1; Mearsheimer, *Conventional Deterrence*; and Biddle, *Military Power*, chap. 3.

communication and artillery ranges as they move forward—such as the distance between Mazar-e-Sharif and Qandahar. Second, defenders use their own artillery fires, making it difficult for attackers to mass and to remain massed for the extended period required to exploit initial success in an attack—the Taliban had employed this tactic in its traditional duel with Northern Alliance troops.[52] Finally, defenders rely on their ability to rapidly bring reserves forward to strengthen their lines at the point of the attack and, equally important, to counterattack enemy forces already weakened by their initial attack. In short, in a combined arms operation, successful defense requires operational communications and mobility. Defenders survive only as long as they can rapidly communicate, move, and counterattack throughout the theater of operations.[53]

Most analyses of the new model have focused on the role of precision bombs on defenders' frontline forces rather than on the other requirements for a successful operational defense. Indeed, precision weapons played an essential role against the frontline forces in both Afghanistan and Iraq. Such weapons are levels of magnitude better at destroying dug-in opponents than artillery. Standard artillery rounds carry only small explosive charges and are not particularly accurate. Although large-scale barrages of shells are good for suppressing infantry, they are not particularly good at destroying them. To kill an entrenched troop, a shell must often land inside the trench or foxhole. Thus, against dispersed opponents taking full advantage of cover, hundreds or even thousands of shells may be required to destroy even a small part of an opposing force.[54]

---

[52] Biddle, *Military Power*, pp. 36-37.

[53] For detailed explanations of the importance of communications, intelligence, and mobility for defenders, see Mearsheimer *Conventional Deterrence*, p. 26; Biddle, *Military Power: Explaining Victory and Defeat in Modern Battle*, p. 32.

[54] See, for instance, Paul Kennedy, "Britain in the First World War," in Allan R. Millett and Williamson Murray, eds., *Military Effectiveness*, (Boston: Allen and Unwin, 1988) Vol. 1.

The same holds true for traditional air bombardment. Precision bombs, on the other hand, contain hundreds or thousands of pounds of explosive and are extremely accurate. A 2,000-pound delayed fuse Joint Direct Attack Munition, for instance, can bury (and kill) all entrenched opponents within a 100-foot diameter of its point of impact and will consistently hit within a few yards of its target. In short, a single bomb can easily be more destructive to entrenched opponents than a sustained artillery barrage.[55] Thus, precision bombs are much more capable than artillery in overcoming tactical defenses and destroying dispersed troops under cover, even without the aid of infantry. In Afghanistan and Iraq, such weapons often made enemies' tactical defenses nearly worthless.[56]

The importance of the air campaign on the theater as a whole however, outweighs the tactical effect of precision weapons on the front lines. In Afghanistan, the Taliban understood the need for operational mobility and had dispersed its troops across the front with the Northern Alliance in a deep network that could be used for mutual support and reinforcement.[57] The U.S. air campaign, however, largely nullified these preparations. From October 7 until the end of the campaign in December, the U.S. conducted a careful bombing campaign against Taliban military forces throughout the theater. U.S. air—and space—born sensors, along with special forces on the ground, proved highly effective at locating and destroying enemy radio and telephone communications and massed enemy

---

[55] Artillery tactics are based on an acknowledgment of this limitation and generally aim to suppress rather than destroy entrenched enemies.

[56] Interview with Maj. Anton Cihak, U.S. Air Force bomber pilot who planned and flew missions in Operation Enduring Freedom. School of Advanced Air and Spaced Studies, November 20, 2004.

[57] The Taliban had deployed its forces throughout the small towns around Mazar-e-Sharif and their environs.

troop concentrations.[58] Within days of the commencement of the campaign, Taliban communications had largely decelerated to the speed of couriers on foot. Troops that were not entrenched had dispersed into small groups that attempted to avoid detection by mixing in with civilians. Movement by Taliban trucks, tanks, and artillery proved deadly. Thus, the Taliban could not concentrate anywhere in the theater and, despite having access to the equipment and tactics of modern war, it was forced to fight as if it did not. In short, the air campaign effectively took out the Taliban's modern equipment and transformed the entire territory under Taliban rule into a kind of front area with no safe terrain where the enemy could freely move, mass, or maintain reserves. The destruction of communications, according to one report, "resulted in a breakthrough and a retreat that turned immediately into an uncontrolled rout."[59]

These dynamics put Taliban troops in a difficult position. On the tactical level, precision weapons put frontline troops on the horns of an impossible dilemma. When the Northern Alliance forces came close enough to spot the Taliban defenses and provide their location to U.S. air assets, bombs quickly destroyed their redoubts. However, if Taliban fighters—who had already dispersed to avoid detection from the air—left their defenses to charge Northern Alliance forces, they faced a more concentrated force that held the tactical advantage of being on the defense and had recourse to precision close air support.[60]

---

[58] Wahid Ahmed, a captured Taliban soldier described the situation on the ground: "We couldn't gather in large groups because that made us a target. We were waiting for our comrades to tell us what to do, but there was nothing to do but hide." Staff Sergeant Jason L. Haag, "OIF Veterans Discuss Lessons," July 31, 2003, *Air Force Link* http://www.af.mil/news/story.asp?storyID=123005347.

[59] Anthony Davis, "How the Afghan War Was Won," *Jane's Intelligence Review*, Vol. 14, No. 2 (February 2002), pp. 8, 11, at p. 11; Interview with Col. Ehrhard.

[60] Interview with Col. Ehrhard.

At least as important, the Taliban's beleaguered forces did not have recourse to the operational-level dynamics necessary to fight a combined arms battle. Although they had constructed the elements of a defense in depth, their communication and movement were too restricted to make use of these defenses—reinforcements were largely nullified.[61] Likewise, they could not bring their artillery to bear on attackers because firing this would expose its location to aerial sensors and subsequent destruction. Conversely, because Northern Alliance forces relied entirely on airpower, they had no significant lines of communication that would become vulnerable to counterattack as their forces moved forward across hundreds of miles of Afghan territory.

When combined, these dynamics had revolutionary effects. Ground forces have long accepted the notion that defense is the stronger form of battle; indeed, classic army doctrine calls for attackers to amass a three-to-one force ratio to succeed against well-prepared defenses. OEF demonstrated that this rule of thumb is no longer valid when air superiority and precision attack are available. Taliban forces outnumbered the Northern Alliance throughout the campaign, often in a ratio of "thousands to hundreds."[62] At Mazar-e-Sharif, for example, more than 5,000 Taliban troops defended the city against some 2,000 Northern Alliance soldiers.[63] In addition to greater numbers and better-

---

[61] Interview with Col. Ehrhard. Biddle provides an account of how this worked in one battle: "At Tarin Kowt on November 18... Taliban forces tried to recapture the village by advancing in a column of vehicles up an exposed road. Frightened AMF [Afghan military forces] . . . defenders were prepared to abandon the village, but precision air strikes called in by American commandos located on an overlooking ridgeline decimated the Taliban column, whose survivors fled the scene in disorder. Taliban reserves ordered forward to reinforce their defenses at Bai Beche were caught moving in the open . . . and were slaughtered by American airpower; officers who surveyed the scene afterward said it brought to mind the infamous 'Highway of Death' leading out of Kuwait City in the 1991 Persian Gulf War." Biddle, "Afghanistan and the Future of Warfare," p. 34. See also, Alastair Finlan "Warfare by Other Means: Special Forces, Terrorism, and Grand Strategy," *Small Wars and Insurgencies*, Vol. 14, No. 1 (Spring 2003), pp. 100-101.

[62] MSgt Bart Decker, correspondence with the authors, January 15, 2004.

[63] Don Chipman, "Air Power and the Battle for Mazar-e Sharif," *Air Power History*, Vol. 50, No. 1 (Spring 2003), pp. 34-45. The campaign for Mazar-e-Sharif consisted of several engagements, so calculating the

trained troops, the Taliban also enjoyed superior firepower, including Soviet artillery and around 450 pieces of armor (including tanks) left over from the Soviet occupation.[64] In contrast, Northern Alliance forces relied almost completely on small arms and traveled mostly on foot or horseback.

Largely due to the numerical imbalance on the ground, the campaign against Mazar-e-Sharif—the closest thing to a front in the war up to that time—had been ineffective in the opening days of OEF. In early November, though, when airpower began to focus on Taliban defenses in the area, the initiative shifted to the rebels—one by one, the cities surrounding Mazar-e-Sharif fell to the Northern Alliance. Throughout, the alliance fought bravely, spearheading attacks on enemy armor with some 1,000 lightly armed fighters on horseback. It was airpower rather than cavalry, however, that turned the tide. In the final assault, the Northern Alliance killed hundreds of Taliban soldiers and captured approximately 3,000 others.[65] More important, the seizure of Mazar-e-Sharif opened a vital land bridge with Uzbekistan, enabling U.S. forces to expand their presence in Afghanistan.

Coalition airpower transformed the Northern Alliance into a lethal fighting force. As one warlord noted, airpower had killed more Taliban in 48 hours with CAS than the Northern Alliance has been able to kill in the previous year.[66] Air force combat controllers, working closely with army SOF and Northern Alliance commanders,

---

force ratio is difficult. The numbers above reflect the forces involved during the final advance on the city. While the numbers are likely low on both sides, the percentages are likely accurate.

[64] Ibid., p. 38.

[65] Dale Andrade, "The Battle For Mazar-e-Sharif October-November 2001," information paper (Washington, US Army Center for Military History, 2002), p. 4.

[66] Col. Tom Entwistle, "Operation Enduring Freedom Preliminary Lessons," Task Force Enduring Look Briefing, chart 22, October 2002.

relentlessly applied airpower to enemy positions and systematically dismantled the Taliban from the air. The action was hardly a victory march, but intense, prolonged combat on the ground was the exception rather than the rule when airpower was available.[67]

In short, new technology available to SOF and airpower transformed the nature of conventional war in Afghanistan. Operations in Afghanistan bore little resemblance to the handful of SOF-based air campaigns of the twentieth century. In those campaigns SOF had played the role of a spoiler, pin pricking enemy forces or destroying valuable but lightly defended targets. In OEF, SOF provided the main effort, using indigenous forces to launch direct attacks on the enemy army's main strength. However, OEF also bore little resemblance to the conventional mass and maneuver warfare of the twentieth century. The Northern Alliance did not need significant rear areas or lines of communication because ground troops did not need to carry their own fire support. The Taliban needed, but did not have access to, safe rear areas or lines of communication. In this type of war, mass and dispersion took on a one-sided aspect. Only the Taliban needed to disperse to avoid artillery fires; because of the new form of air operations, the Northern Alliance could concentrate virtually where and when it pleased. To a large extent, OEF had answered the largest theoretical military debate of the 1990s, demonstrating the unprecedented amount of synergy produced by new airpower technology in conjunction with even feeble ground forces.

---

[67] Exposure to intense combat varied by unit. Interviews with numerous combat controllers suggest that this was a rarity. Key battles at Konduz and Mazar-e-Sharif, for example, featured little to no close combat. Air power routed an attacking column at Tarin Kowt, killing 300 Taliban according to the captured commander, and required no close combat.

Replicating the Afghan model in Iraq

After the fall of the Taliban, academics and politicians alike warned against using the Afghan model as a template for the future, hinting that it could succeed only if the exact circumstances found in Afghanistan were present.[68] Despite the very real possibility of an insurgency in Iraq, and an acrimonious debate behind the scenes, more traditional war planners furiously fought against using the Afghan model in preparing for the looming war in Iraq and eventually won the fight. Although the plan that eventually emerged called for the extensive use of SOF in western Iraq to hunt for SCUD missiles, and in southern Iraq for reconnaissance and stabilization operations, the plan did not call for SOF to work with large bodies of indigenous troops.[69] The pessimists had triumphed. The U.S. would look for local allies after the fighting ended. SOF would work on the periphery; conventional forces would fight conventional forces. As in 2001, planners turned to SOF and airpower only when political circumstances prevented the large-scale deployment of land forces.

The original war plan for Iraqi Freedom called for the entire Fourth Infantry Division to deploy in northern Iraq. Turkey's last-minute refusal to grant staging rights to U.S. ground forces foreclosed this option. In extremis, special forces and airpower were called in and assigned the unenviable mission of replacing an entire infantry

---

[68] Secretary of State Colin Powell, warned in December 2001 that the Afghan model would not work in Iraq: "They're two different countries with two different regimes, two different military capabilities . . . They are so significantly different that you can't take the Afghan model and immediately apply it to Iraq." Quoted in Schmitt and Dao, "Use of Air Power Comes of Age in New War." Milan Vego, writing in July 2002, asserted: "In short, the use of airpower in combination with special forces on the ground can be expected to be successful in some counter terrorist operation or campaign in the future, but not in major regional contingencies." Vego, "What Can We Learn from Enduring Freedom?" Events in Iraq would prove both men wrong.

[69] For descriptions of the roles SOF played in western and southern Iraq, see Linda Robinson, *Masters of Chaos: The Secret History of the Special Forces* (New York, Public Affairs, 2004).

division. Fifty SOF "A" Teams infiltrated northern Iraq with orders to combine forces with the local Kurdish Peshmerga ("those who face death").[70] Using airpower as their main striking force, these fighters would, it was hoped, pin down the thirteen Iraqi divisions on the Green Line,[71] preventing their redeployment to oppose coalition forces advancing on Baghdad from the south.[72]

The campaign in northern Iraq differed in some key aspects from the fighting in Afghanistan. First, the forces on both sides were larger. Kurdish Peshmerga consisted of 50,000 – 70,000 militia troops stationed throughout Northern Iraq. The Iraqi divisions in the north contained 70,000-110,000 regular army and 20,000 Republican Guard troops. Perhaps more important, the need to support the coalition's main thrust from the south restricted the airpower available.[73] Some things, however, remained the same. The Kurd's tactical abilities paled relative to the Iraqi divisions. The Kurds' offensive skills were "nonexistent," often consisting of direct frontal assaults against superior firepower. On the defense, the Kurdish militia was "acceptable" because it had "plenty of practice digging in and establishing a defense after years of anticipating an Iraqi attack."[74] Iraqi

---

[70] A Special Forces Operational Detachment Alpha, or "A" Team, normally consists of twelve personnel.

[71] The "Green Line" was a de facto border within Iraq that roughly separated Kurdish and Iraqi territory

[72] The teams had three primary missions. First, harass the thirteen Iraqi divisions on the Green Line. Second, destroy camps in northern Iraq belonging to the Ansar al-Islam terrorist group. Third, capture key oil fields near Kirkuk and stabilize the northern cities of Mosul and Kirkuk. Williamson Murray and Maj. Gen. Robert H. Scales, Jr., *The Iraq War: A Military History* (Cambridge, Mass.: Belknap Press, 2003), pp. 69-70, 186-190.

[73] Clearly, the Iraqis outnumbered the Kurds, but reliable estimates of the ratio during the war are unavailable. Often, the number of Peshmerga who reported for battle varied widely from the numbers promised by militia leaders. Exact numbers are elusive. See Aysla Aydintasbas, "The Kurdish Dilemma," *Salon.com*, September 6, 2002, http://www.salon.com/people/interview/2002/09/06/salih/; and "Kurdish Resistance Forces Must Decide Role in New Iraq," *Washington Post*, May 13, 2003, available from http://www.charleston.net/stories/051303/ter_13kurds.shtml. ODA Team 391 and 392, for example, were expecting 200 Kurds for an operation, and approximately 80 showed up. See Sean D. Naylor, "Nightmare at Debecka," *Army Times*, September 29, 2003, available from http://www.armytimes.com/archivepaper.php?f=0-ARMYPAPER-2212087.

[74] Capt Joseph Swiecki, correspondence with authors, February 17, 2004.

forces, on the other hand, possessed armor and artillery, which made the lightly armed Kurds extremely vulnerable without air support.

Many details of the operation remain classified, but the experiences of Operational Detachment A Teams 063 and 065 illustrate the potent punch of the SOF/airpower combination. Augmented with highly skilled U.S. Air Force combat controllers and reinforced by as many as 100 Peshmerga, these units engaged in almost continuous combat from March 24 until April 10, 2003.[75] Engagements varied in intensity, but occasionally, the Iraqis applied determined resistance. Air force combat controllers directed close air support missions on all but two days for Team 065, and in eleven out of sixteen of Team 063's engagements.[76] Iraqi defenders generally fought bravely, and success was often far from assured. On April 3, for example, Capt. Eric Carver led his team in a vicious fight:

Advanced with local Peshmerga forces 8 km into enemy division area with one battalion of Saddam Fedayeen and one battalion Republican Guard. Engaged in heavy ground combat . . . with enemy battalion-sized element supported by 120 mm, 82 mm, 60 mm mortars and heavy machine guns and various small arms. Enemy forces tried to launch a counter-attack; members of the team were in direct combat with the enemy. Enemy attack in the morning was fought off with small arms and close air support. Enemy reorganized and mounted another battalion-sized attack in the afternoon again. ODA and Peshmerga forces fought off attack with crew served weapons and small arms. The element was in the process of being flanked when

---

[75] Naylor, "Nightmare at Debecka."

[76] Capt. Eric Carver, U.S. Army, commander, ODA 065, memorandum for record, subject: Historical Documentation of ODA 065 Operations during Operation Iraqi Freedom, Apr 16, 2003. Available from the U.S. Army Center for Army Lessons Learned.

close air support of bombers and strafing runs by F-14s forced the enemy to withdraw to original positions.[77]

Often the Iraqi enemy was larger, better armed, and well motivated.[78] Republican Guard units were also much better trained. U.S. airpower, though, enabled an outnumbered force to remain in contact with the enemy and inflict serious punishment. The commander of ODA 063 observed, "The Kurds were willing to do anything we asked as long as we guaranteed air support."[79]

Operations in Iraq also highlight some of the risks involved with the model. At the battle of Debecka Pass, two SOF teams confronted an entire Iraqi motorized rifle company, including multiple tanks and armored vehicles. Intense enemy artillery fire made this battle a close-run event. Unfortunately, on the first day of the battle, airpower ultimately did more harm than good, as an F-14 jet mistakenly bombed the wrong position, killing seventeen Kurds, and wounding forty others.[80] Low cloud ceilings, a lack of precision ordnance (because many of the aircraft were supporting regular coalition forces in the south), and superior Iraqi armor placement combined to present a challenging target for airpower.[81] After a fierce four and a half hour firefight, courageous

---

[77] Ibid. A battalion-sized element is approximately 1,000 troops.

[78] Baath Party enforcers often inspired enemy motivation. At the battle of Debecka pass, Iraqis attempting to surrender were summarily executed. Interview with Sgt. 1st Class Frank Antenori, Air University, February 18, 2004. See also Murray and Scales, *The Iraq War*, p. 189.

[79] Capt. Joe Swiecki, correspondence with the authors.

[80] Interview with Sgt. 1st Class Frank Antenori.

[81] The Iraqis parked their armor next to an elevated roadway, leaving only the top of the tanks visible to the SF teams. Unfortunately, ground-directed laser energy passed over the turrets due to the "graze" angle generated by a combination of Iraqi placement and friendly troop position. As a result, the laser "spot" impacted the ground well beyond the target. The laser guided bombs functioned properly, but since the laser was not reflecting on the targets, the tanks survived.

U.S. resistance and expert employment of Javelin antitank missiles repelled the Iraqis.[82] The next day, the team fared better: the Iraqis mounted a sizable counterattack, but air strikes forced them to retreat "after the first couple of bombs went off."[83]

Clearly, the use of airpower will not ensure a bloodless victory march for indigenous troops in every situation, and friendly ground forces confronting better-armed and numerically superior enemies run much higher risks if airpower is not available. The salient point, however, is that airpower enabled a numerically inferior force to act decisively in northern Iraq, in spite of occasional setbacks. As one Special Forces team leader related, "Armor or Mechanized Infantry forces could have crushed the northern Iraqi forces, probably faster than we did it; however, the cost would have been significantly more American lives (we lost none). The combination of airpower, SOF, and Kurdish Peshmerga allowed the U.S. to focus ground forces elsewhere, and preserve combat power and American lives."[84]

In Afghanistan and Iraq, the new model helped the United States overcome political and geographical obstacles to produce victory in situations where the preferred forms of force application were impossible. In retrospect, arguments that the model was not replicable were obviously wrong. The new model has quickly become a valuable tool in the U.S. military's arsenal, and has important ramifications for future conflicts. As with any war-fighting doctrine, though, it is not universally applicable, nor is it without limitations.

---

[82] Naylor, "Nightmare at Debecka."

[83] Interview with Sgt. 1st Class Frank Antenori.

[84] Capt. Joe Swiecki, correspondence with the authors.

Understanding the Weakness of the Afghan Model

Although the Afghan model has demonstrated groundbreaking capabilities, two serious, and interrelated, indictments have been leveled against it. Biddle argues that the tactical qualities of the screening force are critical: "Even with precision air support, indigenous allies need a combination of skill, motivation and equipment at least broadly comparable to their enemy's to prevail."[85] Within his framework, skill ranks as the most important factor by far; no other combination of other factors—neither the relative size of the opposing forces nor the technological or material advantage—can compensate for a lack of skill.[86] In a related vein, O'Hanlon argues that the Afghan model is flawed because allied troops will not always be motivated to perform missions required by U.S. campaign plans; U.S. and allied interests will often fail to overlap, with negative results on the battlefield.[87] Both authors use the battles of Tora Bora and Anaconda as case studies to demonstrate these problems.

Although these arguments have some merit, every method in warfare has weaknesses as well as strengths. Obviously the new way of war cannot transform an unruly mob into a force that compares to U.S. standards of training and morale. Nevertheless, Biddle's and O'Hanlon's worries about indigenous allies overstate the problem and do not consider practical solutions and work-arounds. The skill and morale of the indigenous fighting force are important, but it is skill and motivation relative to the plan of operations that matters most—not skill relative to the enemy.

---

[85] Biddle *The Future of Warfare*, p. 43.

[86] In *Military Power*, Biddle presents the theoretical underpinnings of this argument.

[87] O'Hanlon, "A Flawed Masterpiece."

TORA BORA

The problems the Afghan model encountered at the battle of Tora Bora have been the most cited evidence of the model's weaknesses. Critics have relentlessly pointed to the inability of the United States' Afghan allies to capture bin Laden and his followers in that battle—bin Laden was not found and most of the al-Qaida combatants in the area fought to the death or escaped. The popular media and numerous analysts have argued that the United States' Afghan allies lacked the skill and motivation to accomplish the mission assigned to them and that, consequently, the Afghan model itself is unreliable and cannot substitute for U.S. troops using conventional tactics.[88]

This interpretation of events is only half right. At the battle of Tora Bora, the United States' Afghan allies certainly lacked the skill and motivation to accomplish the mission assigned to them, but this fact demonstrated a flaw in U.S. planning rather than in the ability of proxy forces. As we show below, the objectives for the Afghans laid out by U.S. war planners were so difficult that even a highly motivated, well-trained, and well-equipped modern army would have had trouble accomplishing them. Judging the Afghan model against this standard is a mistake. A better standard would be how well airpower and proxy forces did at digging entrenched al-Qaida fighters from their caves, a mission that was successful.

After the Taliban regime collapsed, surviving al-Qaida forces retreated to the mountain fortress of Tora Bora. Relative to the Taliban forces the allies had faced up to this point, the enemy at Tora Bora was made up mostly of better trained al-Qaida forces,

---

[88] Smucker, *al qaida's Great Escape.* See also Arostegui, "The Search for bin Laden"; Biddle, *Special Forces and the Future of Warfare*; Donnelly, "Fighting Terror/The Military Campaign"; Glasser, "The Battle of Tora Bora:"; and O'Hanlon, "A Flawed Masterpiece."

tactically superior to the United States' Afghan allies. Beyond this, the U.S. and Northern Alliance goals began to diverge. By this point the alliance had conquered more of Afghanistan's territory than it could easily control. Northern Alliance warlords saw little gain in a campaign of extermination against al-Qaida. The United States, on the other hand, was transfixed by intelligence that placed bin Laden in the area of Tora Bora and apprehensive about the possibility that even a small number of al-Qaida fighters might survive to carry out more acts of terror against U.S. targets.[89]

The U.S. military plan consisted of two basic elements: first, airpower would pummel the cave complexes in hopes of dislodging the enemy. Second, thousands of Afghans would exploit the results of the bombing by fighting cave-to-cave and by providing a "backstop" to prevent the enemy from fleeing to Pakistan. Next to destroying the enemy, the most important part of the mission was capturing members of al-Qaida.[90] Why planners thought that this might be possible given al-Qaida's history of fighting to the death remains unclear.[91]

Conditions at Tora Bora awed military planners: most of the fighting took place above 10,000 feet in some of the world's most rugged terrain. One U.S. Army adviser reported, "You have to see it to believe it. I personally conducted a recon up to 9,000 feet and I was still in the foothills. Steep peaks, deep valleys, small foot trails, and that

[89] Smucker, *al qaida's Great Escape*; Sean Naylor, *Not a Good Day to Die: The Untold Story of Operation Anaconda* (New York: Berkley Books, 2005), p. 19.

[90] Brooks, et al., *The First Year*, p. 34, and Richard Stewart, "The US Army in Afghanistan: October 2001 – March 2002," US Army Center for Military History pamphlet, June 24, 2004, p. 24.

[91] Before he was assassinated by al-Qaida, Massoud, the former leader of the Northern Alliance, related that he had never managed to capture a member of al Qaida because they consistently killed themselves when facing imminent capture. Woodward, *Bush at War*, p. 52.

was the good part."[92] Large numbers of Taliban and al-Qaida fighters had fortified already-favorable defensive positions, and stockpiled supplies and ammunition. As U.S. Army historian Richard Stewart observes, "Tora Bora appeared to be an extremely tough target.[93]

In spite of the challenging conditions, the lack of conventional military units forced U.S. planners to rely on indigenous troops for the attack on Tora Bora.[94] The force tapped for this difficult operation, however, was ill prepared. One Afghan leader noted, "When we started off in Tora Bora, we didn't have enough real information . . . but the Americans were in a big hurry to start the offensive. We had a force there, but we didn't have a good enough intelligence network."[95] In addition, local fighters arrived at Tora Bora with little preparation and inadequate equipment. One Afghan leader recalls "I only heard about the offensive that day at 7 A.M. . . . My father told me, 'just go,' so I . . . took 700 soldiers. We got there, but I don't know for what. We had no food or anything."[96] In many cases, these troops proved unreliable, allegedly accepting bribes from al-Qaida fighters in return for safe passage.[97] One man admitted that he had taken "20 important Arabs into Pakistan."[98]

---

[92] Lt. Col. Christopher Haas, U.S. Army Special Forces adviser to the Afghans, personal correspondence, February 18, 2004. Another adviser called it, "the most formidable terrain that we fought in." Naylor, p. 19.

[93] Stewart, "The US Army in Afghanistan."

[94] U.S. Marines had established a small forward base near Kandahar, and only a reinforced company of the 10th Mountain Division was available at Bagram and Mazar-e-Sharif. See ibid.

[95] Quoted in Glasser, "The Battle of Tora Bora."

[96] Ibid.

[97] "Hazrat Ali is very opportunistic, taking money from our side, and also the al qaida folks," according to an unnamed Western diplomat, quoted in ibid.

[98] Donnelly, "Fighting Terror/The Military Campaign."

The results of the operation at Tora Bora were predictable: "A few Al Qaeda were captured, but most of them fought to the death or slipped away into the relative safety of nearby Pakistan. The whereabouts of Osama bin Laden, or even whether he had been in the Tora Bora region in the first place remained a mystery."[99] In the aftermath of this failure, most criticism focused on the skill of the indigenous allies. A British Special Air Services officer described a popular view of the outcome: "The idea was for native troops to provide a blocking force who were simply not up to the task."[100]

Probably more important than skill, however, was Afghan morale. Understanding the motivation of the indigenous ally is a critical consideration in proxy warfare. Most Afghans were unaware of the terrorist attacks of September 11 and would not have been tremendously concerned by them if they had known. In essence, the Afghans had little quarrel with al-Qaida—their enemy was the Taliban. Once the Taliban fell, the meaning of the war changed for the rebels. As one RAND analyst observes, "The Afghans didn't have much enthusiasm for fighting Al Qaeda in the post-Taliban era."[101] Local commanders, accustomed to years of factional infighting, were reportedly "reluctant" to pursue the enemy into the White Mountains, "preferring instead to stay in newly liberated Jalalabad to stake out their own turf."[102]

Yet, despite the disincentives for Afghans to fight at Tora Bora, U.S. liaisons convinced their allies to fight. This was not always easy, as one army SF adviser to the

---

[99] Stewart, "The US Army in Afghanistan," p. 26.

[100] Quoted in Arostegui, "The Search for bin Laden."

[101] Interview with Bruce Pirnie, RAND analyst, School of Advanced Air and Space Studies, Maxwell Air Force Base, Alabama, October 22, 2003.

[102] Donnelly, "Fighting Terror/The Military Campaign." In addition, Lt. Col. Christopher Haas and Col. Mark Rosengard confirmed this. Haas, correspondence; interview with Rosengard, February 27, 2004; Naylor, p. 19.

Afghans explains, "On numerous occasions, I had to personally sit down and negotiate with [Afghan] General Hazrat Ali and convince him to stay in the fight."[103] To strengthen the Afghan's commitment at Tora Bora, U.S. officials paid the warlords cash bonuses, ranging from $30,000 for supplies to perhaps as much as "several hundred thousand dollars" in return for their support.[104] Thus, at Tora Bora, Afghan morale was built on U.S. diplomacy and cash, not internal motivation. Nevertheless, the Afghans fought.

Troop motivation is a critical factor in war, and it becomes more important as combat conditions grow more dangerous. Afghan commanders had good reasons for wanting to avoid Tora Bora. They had successfully held off the Soviets in this area, and they had an intimate understanding of the difficulty inherent in fighting in the White Mountains. The challenging operation even led U.S. Marine Corps leaders to refuse the opportunity to commit forces at that time.[105] At Tora Bora, extreme altitudes and "unbelievable" terrain led to conditions that wholly favored the enemy. Assertions that "bombing without energetic ground exploitation" led to al-Qaida's escape at Tora Bora ignore the enormity of the task.[106] A British special forces unit charged with clearing one of the caves in the area called it "one of the most daring engagements that the 22 SAS (Special Air Service) Regiment has undertaken in 30 years."[107] According to U.S. Army Col. Mark Rosengard, director of operations for Task Force Dagger, "You can't find the

---

[103] Haas, correspondence.

[104] Donnelly, "Fighting Terror/The Military Campaign."

[105] Lt. Col. Haas relates that the enormity of the task presented a logistical and tactical problem that the Marines were unwilling to tackle at this stage of the war. Haas, correspondence.

[106] Stephen Biddle, "Why the Taliban Fell," PowerPoint briefing, June 6, 2002, slide 13.

[107] Quoted in, Finlan, "Warfare by Other Means," p. 102.

infantry organization in anybody's army that can occupy and control Tora Bora."[108] As a result, "Air power and eyes on the ground identifying [enemy] locations [were] not only key but the only way we killed bad guys."[109]

Operations at Tora Bora were difficult, dangerous, and most important, part of the United States' war against al-Qaida. As a result, Afghan commanders had little real interest in the outcome. As the mayor of Jalalabad, a veteran mujahiddeen, noted, "They are just doing these things for the money."[110]

Far from showing that the critics of the Afghan model are correct, however, the desperate lack of preparation and the low morale of the Afghans at Tora Bora underscores the model's resiliency. In the battle a poorly trained, unmotivated Afghan force screened U.S. troops and assaulted prepared positions against a well-trained, highly motivated opponent dug into one of the most defensible places on the planet. Despite the unfavorable odds, U.S. airpower and Afghan allies rapidly routed the force and drove it from the region. Neither inferior tactical skill nor abysmal morale had much effect on this aspect of the battle. Despite successfully using the area as a redoubt against the Soviets, Osama bin Laden apparently decided that he could not hold out against the Americans.[111]

---

[108] Interview with Rosengard; Naylor, p. 19. Haas adds, "Even our best [infantry divisions] would have had serious, serious difficulties in this area." Haas, correspondence.

[109] Haas, correspondence.

[110] Donnelly, "Fighting Terror/The Military Campaign." Haas notes that Ali's main motivation came from money, television coverage, and the prestige associated with U.S. support. Ibid.

[111] Hastert, "Operation Anaconda," pp. 13-14.

Nevertheless, many critics overlook this success to focus blame on the use of

Afghan troops for the United States' failure to capture or kill bin Laden at Tora Bora.[112]

Armed with a better understanding for the difficulty of the task, it is clear that hopes that

the plan would succeed at Tora Bora were overly optimistic. As the battle of Anaconda

later demonstrated, given the conditions in Afghanistan, capturing enemy leaders would

be too difficult for even highly trained troops to accomplish.

ANACONDA AND THE NEED FOR THOROUGH PLANNING

Two months after the battle of Tora Bora, coalition intelligence located a large group of

al-Qaida in the Shah-e-Khot valley. Based on the perceived failures at Tora Bora, the

Afghan model was scrapped in favor of a new set of tactics. The plan differed from the

earlier approach in two main ways. First, it called for airpower to play a minor role,

rather than to be the main effort as it had been in operations up to this point. This

alteration in the basic template to date in Afghanistan was based on the fear that heavy

use of air to prepare the battlefield would cause the enemy to flee and that, as at Tora

Bora, the operation would result in few captives.[113] The second main difference was the

role of the allied Afghans in the battle. This time, rather than acting as light infantry

screeners, the Afghans were to be shock troops in a "hammer and anvil" operation. By

this time, the enemy was relying on the tactic of blending into local civilian populations.

---

[112] There are few examples of enemy leaders being captured during war. The preeminent one is probably Napoleon III, who was captured at Sedan during the Franco-Prussian War. A number of variables contribute to the likelihood of a leader being captured including: terrain, friendly local population, and the absence of friendly forces in the area. At Tora Bora, such factors strongly favored al Qaida leaders escaping. Both Rosengard and Haas assert that U.S. Army planners were unsurprised by the Afghans' failure at Tora Bora. Rosengard notes, "just the fact that he [Ali] got us to that piece of ground was a success." Haas, correspondence; and interview with Rosengard.

[113] Lt. Gen. Hagenbeck, Joint Task Force commander, Operation Enduring Freedom, interviewed by Maj. Mark Davis in Washington, D.C., January 28, 2004.

Based, in part, on the belief that Afghans would be better than Americans at distinguishing enemies from noncombatants, as well as the availability of Afghan troops, the plan called for allied Afghans to perform the difficult task of dislodging the enemy from villages at the base of the Shah-e-Khot valley and to drive them against a U.S. Army "anvil."[114]

The attack went poorly from the beginning. Ground-air planning was next to non-existent.[115] Despite the decision not to use airpower to soften up enemy positions, the enemy was warned and in defensive positions. When the Afghans began the attack, they encountered numerous problems then came under heavy fire, suffered casualties, and retreated.[116] With the "hammer" out of the picture, al-Qaida defenders turned their attention on the U.S. anvil, engaging hundreds of U.S. troops in one of the longest American firefights since Vietnam. The battle was at least a partial coalition victory: al-Qaida forces were driven from the valley, and an estimated 500 enemy were killed.[117] This success was incomplete, however, as perhaps two-thirds of the enemy combatants slipped through the U.S. blocking force using numerous "rat trails" out of the mountains.[118]

---

[114] U.S. forces were chosen for the "anvil" role specifically because it was believed they had the skill to perform the job and because it was feared that, in a repeat of Tora Bora, Afghans could be bribed to allow the enemy to escape. Naylor, pp. 118-120.

[115] For a description of the problems see: *Operation Anaconda An Air Power Perspective*, United States Air Force Headquarters AF/XOL, 2005.

[116] "Operation Anaconda Case Study" (Maxwell AFB, AL: College of Aerospace Doctrine, Research, and Education, 2003), p. 26; Naylor, pp. 184-189, 197-206. Although not known at the time, the Afghan force also suffered "friendly fire" from an AC-130 on the scene.

[117] Eight U.S. troops died in action during Operation Anaconda. Interestingly, these troops were part of a separate operation outside the direct control of the main U.S. commander, then Maj. Gen. Franklin "Buster" Hagenbeck. Hastert, "Operation Anaconda," pp. 15-18.

[118] U.S. Air Force intelligence estimates placed the number of fighters in the valley at 1500. The U.S. Army claims some 500 enemy combatants were killed in Operation Anaconda. Naylor puts the enemy losses at 150-300, Naylor, pp. 375-376.

Allied soldiers faced challenging conditions in Anaconda. Much like Tora Bora, the terrain favored the enemy. In addition, the Afghans had the difficult task of advancing on enemy villages protected by interlocking fire with little terrain protection. U.S. planners had sound reasons for using their Afghan allies in this way, but any judgment of Afghan performance at Anaconda must be tempered by the knowledge that, like the U.S. air force, Afghan leaders were not included in operational planning for Anaconda, even though their forces constituted a critical portion of the effort. [119]

Out of fear that mixed Afghan loyalties might compromise the operation, Northern Alliance leaders learned the details of Operation Anaconda only seventy-two hours before it was to commence.[120] Obviously, U.S. commanders faced a difficult choice; including the Afghans in the planning process risked potentially jeopardizing operational security and American lives. This decision, however, left Afghan forces (and their U.S. advisers) with little time to prepare for a difficult battle. The effect of this late notice on the Afghans is hard to calculate. In light of the difficult tactical task presented them, their limited fighting skills, and the lack of preparation time, it seems reasonable to assume that the Northern Alliance was less than optimally prepared for battle.[121]

---

[119] According to Army Col. David Gray, one of Operation Anaconda's key planners, the U.S. planned to use the Afghan force in this situation for three reasons: (1) to appear different from previous Soviet incursions into the area, (2) to project the notion that the U.S. was "helping the Afghans help themselves," and (3) the U.S. needed the Afghans to perform the difficult task of separating enemy combatants from civilians in the villages. For more on the reasons the air force was not included in the planning process see Elaine Grossman, "Was Operation Anaconda Ill-Fated From Start? Army Analyst Blames Afghan Battle Failings On Bad Command Set-Up." *Inside The Pentagon*, July 29, 2004.

[120] Interview with Rosengard.

[121] An acrimonious debate persists over why the air force was not fully included in the planning for Anaconda. For a discussion of this debate see Davis, "Operation Anaconda: Command and Confusion in Joint Warfare," master's thesis, School of Advanced Air and Space Studies, Maxwell Air Force Base, Alabama, 2004).

Excluding key units from planning, notifying them of the operation at the last minute, and denying them the opportunity to train for the mission at hand are hardly recipes for tactical success—in any army. Anaconda also highlights an important point: fog and friction will have greater effects on poorly trained forces. Accordingly, any plan that depends on expert performance by indigenous untrained allies should be considered suspect.[122]

In the end, the Afghans did return to the battle and, in conjunction with U.S. forces defeated the al-Qaida fighters. Increasingly the battle evolved from an old model combined arms operation to one in which U.S. and friendly Afghan forces pinned down al-Qaida troops with small arms fire and relied on airpower to destroy the enemy—that is, despite all planning to the contrary, increasingly it came to look like the Afghan model. In the face of hundreds of skilled U.S. troops attempting to block their escape, as at Tora Bora, a large number of al-Qaida fighters got away. Despite the skill and morale of U.S. forces, the outcome was the same as Tora Bora. Anaconda revealed a number of weaknesses in the Afghan model, but more than anything else, it demonstrated the relative efficacy of the tactics used throughout the earlier portion of the campaign.

SKILL AND MORALE.

Although critics use the fighting at Tora Bora and Operation Anaconda to demonstrate the shortcomings of the Afghan model, in reality these highlight the fact that indigenous allies are not strict substitutes for U.S. infantry and military planners must work around their limitations on a case-by-case basis. In Afghanistan, the critical attribute of the Afghan rebels was often that they were willing to fight. As Colonel Rosengard observes,

_____

[122] Naylor, pp. 144-145.

the primary qualification required of the Afghans at Anaconda was "that they could physically pick up a rifle and move toward the objective." At Tora Bora, "just the fact that [the allies] got us [the Americans] to that piece of ground was a success."[123] Indigenous allies will not normally perform as well as U.S. troops: U.S. advisers must design strategies that match the ally's capabilities to U.S. objectives. Rosengard sums up the nature of proxy warfare: "If you gain credibility with an indigenous force and you bring a capability he doesn't have, he can achieve what he wants, and we can achieve what we want. It's a two-way street, and it's often only good for today, not necessarily for tomorrow. The weakness is in the analysis of where those needs align . . . and that's on us."[124]

Thus, the skill of the allies is relevant, but it is skill relative to the plan that matters most. If Biddle were right, and tactical skill relative to the enemy is necessary for airpower to make a difference, the presence of U.S. troops at Anaconda should have produced much better results than at Tora Bora. Unfortunately, although the enemy body count may have been higher at Anaconda, the strategic result was the same: the battle ended when the enemy decided to leave. To pin this strategic failure on the Afghan allies is to obscure a lack of effective U.S. planning.

When operations require complex fire and maneuver, the ally's tactical skill will indeed be critical. When the ally's role is simply to fix the enemy in place, motivation will be more important than skill. Using indigenous forces to defeat the Taliban or to harass the Iraqis on the Green Line is a far different proposition than using the new model to fight a modern army. The circumstances required for success using the new model

---

[123] Interview with Rosengard.

[124] Ibid; Naylor, pp. 144-145.

will vary depending on a host of factors. Expecting an untrained force to be successful using traditional U.S. doctrine and battle plans is a mistake. Leaders must plan custom solutions to unique problems—hardly a shocking revelation in the annals of warfare.

Strategic Implications of the Afghan model

To this point we have focused mainly on tactical questions and argued that the pessimism of earlier analyses is significantly overstated; the Afghan model has proven capable of defeating both conventional and guerrilla forces. When the proxy forces' limitations are recognized and considered in planning operations, the model is replicable under substantially different conditions and has shown itself to work even when less skilled proxy forces are deployed against more skilled enemies and when proxy forces have little or no political motivation to fight for U.S. goals. Examining only the tactical issues associated with the new model, however, obscures its true value. After all, if the value of the new model was measured simply in terms of a comparison of the military capability of proxy forces and a heavy deployment of U.S. troops, it would clearly come up wanting. The importance of new model comes from its strategic value.

MILITARY CREDIBILITY

According to a well-known formula, a country's military power combines its physical capability to fight and its willingness to bear the costs associated with that capability.[125] All the capability in the world is worthless if a leader is unwilling to marshal it for fear of casualties.

---

[125] See, for instance, Glen H. Snyder and Paul Diesing, *Conflict among Nations: Bargaining, Decision Making, and System Structure in International Crises* (Princeton, N.J.: Princeton University Press, 1977); Zeev Maoz, "Resolve, "Capabilities and the Outcomes of Interstate Disputes," *Journal of Conflict Resolution* Vol. 26, No. 2 (June 1983), pp. 195-230; Russell J. Leng, *Interstate Crisis Behavior, 1816-1980: Realism versus Reciprocity* (New York: Cambridge University Press, 1993).

For the United States, the new model significantly reduces the costs associated with war. In both Afghanistan and Iraq, small numbers of special forces teams carried out missions that military planners had previously believed would involve heavy divisions of U.S. forces, tens of billions of dollars, and significant U.S. casualties.[126] While the missions were not without costs or casualties, success came at a relatively low cost compared to using traditional conventional forces and tactics.

Beyond the fear of casualties, using a proxy force also allows U.S. commanders to attempt more aggressive operations. As Captain Swiecki observed after operations in northern Iraq: "Conventional forces would not have accepted the unfavorable force ratios or the risks we took. We were able to take such risks because we were risking mainly Kurdish lives (sounds bad, but true), and we had faith in our ability to effectively use airpower, or slip away if things went dangerously wrong (we were only eight Americans). American troops would not risk a movement to contact against an enemy with greater numbers and better equipment with only a trust in airpower and Iraqi cowardice to even the odds."[127]

Nor could the U.S. military easily replicate these types of operations with its own light forces. In both Afghanistan and Iraq, once the pattern of the new model became apparent, enemy forces began to respond with quasi-guerrilla tactics, dispersing into small units and hiding. Ground forces in this configuration were difficult to detect from the air; often the only way to find them was to wait until they began shooting at the screening force. Airpower was then called in to destroy the hidden enemy. As the U.S.

---

[126] Woodward, *Bush at War*, p. 43. For an earlier analysis of the requirements for this mission, see Benjamin and Simon, *The Age of Sacred Terror*, p. 295.

[127] Swiecki, correspondence.

learned in Vietnam, in rough terrain, this type of warfare can produce large numbers of casualties. Current experiences in Iraq suggest this is equally true of wars fought in urban environments.[128]

Such a capability, some would argue, could make war too easy for the United States; that when war costs too few lives America will resort to it too quickly.[129] Although there is something to this argument, there is also another side. When presented with an option that seems too costly, leaders will react by doing nothing. In 1998, after al-Qaida bombed the U.S. embassies in Kenya and Tanzania, President Bill Clinton asked the Pentagon for options for putting "boots on the ground" in Afghanistan and was particularly interested in SOF options. Gen. Henry H. "Hugh" Shelton, chairman of the Joint Chiefs, quickly dismissed the possibility of a SOF campaign and, based on a standard conventional model, outlined a campaign that required months of preparation, and tens of thousands of U.S. troops. Based on the high costs of this plan, Shelton dismissed the political feasibility of any Afghan campaign and the president, left with no low-cost alternative, was forced to agree.[130] It is at least possible that a SOF campaign in 1998 would have prevented the September 11 attacks. Thus, while making war too cheap has the possibility of leading the U.S. into wars it would otherwise avoid, avoiding war out of casualty aversion is not always a wise choice. Using indigenous ground forces, with a small number of special operations units on the ground and airpower, offers the United States an opportunity to use military power, increasing the strategic utility of armed force.

---

[128] For the use of SOF heavy methods without indigenous allies, see Robinson, *Masters of Chaos*, chap. 9.
[129] For an elegant exposition of this argument see Andrew J. Bacevich, *American Empire* (Cambridge, Mass.: Harvard University Press, 2002).

[130] Benjamin and Simon, *The Age of Sacred Terror*, p. 294-5

INDIGENOUS FORCES AND GUERRILLA WAR

A second argument in favor of the new model involves avoiding the problem of an insurgency. Today, U.S. conventional power vastly exceeds that of any likely conventional enemy; however, the U.S. military has proven vulnerable to guerrilla tactics.[131] In the lead-up to the war in Afghanistan, both U. S. policy makers and al-Qaida's leaders predicted that sending large contingents of U.S. troops into a Muslim country would result in a protracted guerrilla war.

The congruence of predictions between these two groups about the likely results of a U.S. invasion of Afghanistan is not hard to fathom and stems from the nature of guerrilla war. Thinkers as diverse as Mao Zedong and U.S. Army doctrine writers agree that the center of gravity in a guerrilla war resides in the population. Mao characterized the relationship between the local population and the fighters as water to fish, and he stressed the need to go to extraordinary lengths to maintain the people's good will.[132] Similarly, the U.S. Army field manual on guerrilla war points out the importance of continuous moral and material support from the civilian population for the success of a guerrilla movement.[133] Foreign soldiers acting as police are unlikely to endear themselves to the local population, particularly when they do not share the local language and do not understand the local customs. Nor is simple firepower likely to be enough. The United States' experience in Vietnam, France's experience in Vietnam and Algeria, and the Soviet Union's experience in Afghanistan suggest that, when facing a committed

---

[131] The current insurgency in Iraq as well as the United State's experience in the Vietnam War and the Soviet Union's experience in the Afghan War highlight the vulnerability of great powers to guerrilla warfare.

[132] See Mao Tse-Tung, *On Guerrilla War*, trans. Samuel B. Griffith (Fort Bragg, N.C.: Army Special Warfare School, 1989), chap 6.

[133] FM 31-21 Department of the Army Field Manual, Guerrilla Warfare and Special Forces Operations.

local population, even inflicting hundreds of thousands or millions of casualties upon them may not be enough to win.

A strong case can be made that the U.S. experiences in Afghanistan and Iraq prove this point. In Afghanistan, where Afghan troops made up the bulk of the occupying forces, the insurgency is limited. This is particularly remarkable considering the makeup of the political map at the time the Taliban regime fell. Perhaps the strongest political fault lines in Afghanistan run between the Northern Alliance's ethnic Tajik and Uzbeks and the ethnic Pashtuns in the south.[134] When the war ended, Northern Alliance forces occupied the country from its northern border to Qandahar, a situation almost certain to result in serious political and military conflict between the conquerors and conquered.[135] Nevertheless, based on the type of political compromise and negotiation that is only possible between opponents who have an intimate understanding of each other's political and military situation, a compromise was reached. The compromise was greatly aided by the Northern Alliance's knowledge that the United States would not continue to support them if they exceeded their mandate. Local leaders were quickly found to govern newly liberated populations and, by and large, the local population was left to follow its ancient customs and laws.

Interestingly, a similar process occurred in Northern Iraq where the United States had relied on Kurds as its primary ground force and to police liberated territory. The only area in northern Iraq that experienced significant violence during the insurgency has been Mosul. Mosul is also the only portion of that area in which U.S. forces took a direct

---

[134] Throughout the campaign the fear of civil war between these factions was a major consideration in NSC planning. Woodward, *Bush at War*, p. 187.

[135] Peter Beaumont, et al., "The Rout of the Taliban." See also Woodward, *Bush at War*, p. 187.

hand in political administration. Although it would be easy to overstate the case in this region, because most of the policed population in northern Iraq is Kurdish, it is still interesting to note how smoothly the transition went in comparison to regions in the south where the United States did not use proxies and attempted to police the local populations itself.

Although proxy forces are not always available, when they are, and particularly when they speak the same language and adhere to the same institutions as the conquered population, they are more likely to be greeted as liberators than are U.S. troops.[136] Because the new model does not rely on large numbers of U.S. ground forces, the United States is more likely to be seen as an able partner than an occupying force. By fighting on the side of the Afghans and the Kurds, the U.S. helped solidify post-conflict support and minimized the chances of armed conflict with these factions. Had the U.S. attempted to fight in Afghanistan without the Northern Alliance, or in Iraq without the Kurds, it would have increased the chances that these factions would be actively opposing U.S. presence in their countries rather than cooperating in rebuilding efforts.

CREDIBILITY AND DIPLOMACY

A third argument for the new model—really an implication of the first two—is that it has the potential to strengthen U.S. diplomacy. Empirical work on U.S. diplomatic coercion has demonstrated a disturbing pattern. The United States' enemies have a tendency to discount its military threats. According to Robert Art and Patrick Cronin, for instance, the United States achieved its goals through coercive diplomacy in less than a third of its

---

[136] See Babak Dehghanpisheh, "Now We Have America," *Newsweek,* April 7, 2003, p. 35, http://search.epnet.com/direct.asp?an=9406938&db=aph.

attempts.[137] In the other cases, coercive diplomacy failed, forcing the U.S. to go to war to obtain its goals or simply to abandon them. A generation has been shaped by memories of U.S. forces retreating from places such as Vietnam, Lebanon, and Somalia; and of seemingly meaningless air strikes on places such as Laos, Cambodia, Libya, Iraq, Sudan, and Afghanistan. These lessons have not been lost on the United States' enemies. Both Saddam Hussein and Osama bin Laden repeatedly cited such cases to inspire their followers to resist U.S. demands.[138] Their simple, and largely accurate, argument has been that the United States will not spend the lives of its people fighting for goals as abstract as opposing terrorism or preventing unfriendly regimes from obtaining nuclear weapons.

More recently another argument about U.S. power has emerged. Since mid-2004, as the insurgency in Iraq grew, Iran has repeatedly rebuffed U.S. demands that it end its nuclear program. In January 2005, Iran's President Khatami publicly stated that he did not fear the United States because of its vulnerability to insurgency as demonstrated in Iraq.[139] There is much truth to this analysis of U.S. policy. As long as the U.S. way of war requires U.S. troops to occupy foreign soil, the chances of an insurgency are high. As long as foreign leaders understand this dynamic, they have little reason to back down in the face of U.S. military threats. Against threats of the Afghan model, however, Iran would have more to fear. As is the case with many autocratic countries, Iran possesses armed dissident groups (Kurds, Baluchs, and various pro-democratic Persian groups).

---

[137] Robert J. Art and Patrick M. Cronin, *The United States and Coercive Diplomacy*, (Washington D.C.: United States Institute of Peace Press, 2003), Chap. 9.

[138] See Zimmerman, "Strategic Provocation," p. 49.

[139] As regards a U.S. attack he stated, "The possibility of a U.S. attack against Iran is very low. We think America is not in a position to take a lunatic action of attacking Iran....The U.S. is deeply engaged in Iraq." *Baltimore Sun*, January 21, 2005.

Supported by U.S. SOF and airpower, these groups would be formidable levers to use in a war; and a potential way of sidestepping the problem of occupation. Similar dynamics are likely to apply in Syria, Sudan, and other states with regimes hostile to the United States. Because their leaders are aware that such operations are relatively cheap for the U.S., threats based on the Afghan model will often be more credible.

Conclusion

Dramatic changes in the military capability of the United States offer a way to alter the dynamics of U.S. foreign policy. In Operation Enduring Freedom and along Operation Iraqi Freedom's northern front, a handful of highly skilled SOF personnel bridged the gap between the world's premier air force and indigenous allies. These unlikely alliances toppled the Taliban regime, destroyed Saddam's military power in northern Iraq, and provided these regions with a chance for stable democracy. After conducting two extremely successful campaigns using the new model, the U.S. military would do well to stop ignoring its potential. Future planners must consider the model as a primary option, rather than an emergency procedure.

Critics of the Afghan model focus most of their attention on tactical limitations. Some argue that the new technological capabilities embodied in precision airpower and global positioning systems are of limited utility in the field. Others postulate that indigenous allies must possess tactical skill equal to or greater than their enemy's. We have argued that the strategic benefits of fighting by proxy outweigh the costs created by proxies' limited tactical skill. Tactical skill remains a relevant consideration, but it is skill relative to the plan of operations that matters most. By designing plans to maximize their ally's unique capabilities and limitations rather than simply substituting plans designed for highly skilled U.S. troops, U.S. planners can achieve victory.

Undoubtedly the strategic context for Afghanistan and Iraq differed, although the end result ended up much the same. In Afghanistan, the U.S. objective was to eliminate Al Qaeda, in Iraq to overthrow Saddam Hussein's regime. While overthrowing the Taliban was not necessary to achieving the original objective in Afghanistan, in the end this is in fact what occurred, reducing the differences between the two wars. Just as tactical planners must carefully consider how to utilize indigenous forces, strategic planners must judiciously utilize the new model. As Biddle observed, the model "can work under some important preconditions, but those preconditions will not always be present."[140] Planners must consider the objectives sought before deciding to implement the Afghan model. If the objective is to invade and conquer a well-defended country possessing a modern, first-rate military, the model is not likely to work. If, however, the objective is to coerce or overthrow an enemy regime with less military capability, in some circumstances the model will work admirably. As a result, the new model has important ramifications for U.S. foreign policy.

The new model helps bridge the gap between the United States' realist aspirations and its liberal ideals by allowing indigenous allies to do the bulk of fighting and dying to achieve their own freedom. Allowing the local ally to shoulder the bulk of the fighting helps legitimize post conflict political activity, and enhances the prospects for long-term success. Had the United States forsaken its proxies in Afghanistan and used its own large-scale conventional forces, it is probable that many of the dissident Afghan factions currently bickering about the nature of their government would be mounting an

---

[140] Biddle, "Afghanistan and the Future of Warfare," p. 49.

insurgency against the United States.

The pessimism over the Afghan model has been misplaced. The model represents an important, even revolutionarily, new tool in the United States' foreign policy arsenal. Ultimately, the model allowed the U.S. military to substitute a handful of airpower, SOF and local allies for tens of thousands of American troops in the last two wars. This is economy of force in its purest form. The innovative application of this system in the past two campaigns allowed the Bush administration the opportunity to depose two distasteful, authoritarian regimes in less than two years, and sent a powerful signal to would-be adversaries. At least as significantly, because it does not require the United States to unilaterally occupy the territory it conquers, the model is much less likely than conventional methods of war to embroil the United States in guerrilla wars. In short, in future coercive diplomacy and war, the Afghan model should enjoy a prestigious place in the United States' foreign policy toolkit.